Breakfast Blast

Bobbie Kalman

 Crabtree Publishing Company

www.crabtreebooks.com

Created by Bobbie Kalman

For my dear friend Sam Graci,
whose chats about nutrition have finally found a home!

Author and Publisher
Bobbie Kalman

Editorial director
Niki Walker

Editor
Kathryn Smithyman

Copy editors
Molly Aloian
Laura Hysert

Art director
Robert MacGregor

Design
Bobbie Kalman
Katherine Kantor
Samantha Crabtree

Production coordinator
Heather Fitzpatrick

Digital prepress
Embassy Graphics

Special thanks
Margaret Nacsa, Sophie Izikson, Martin Izikson, Sara Paton,
Alexis Gaddishaw, Robin Turner, David Kanters, Andrew Key,
Chantelle Styres, and Jacquelyn Labonté

Consultants
Valerie Martin, Registered Nutrition Consultant,
    International Organization of Nutrition Consultants
Ellen Brown, Founding Food Editor of USA Today
    and author of several best-selling cookbooks

Food preparation
Valerie Martin
Kathryn Smithyman
Margaret Nacsa
Samantha Crabtree

Photographs
All photographs by Bobbie Kalman
Other images by PhotoDisc, Comstock, and Digital Stock

Illustrations
All illustrations by Barbara Bedell

Printer
Worzalla Publishing

Crabtree Publishing Company
www.crabtreebooks.com   1-800-387-7650

PMB 16A
350 Fifth Avenue
Suite 3308
New York, NY
10118

612 Welland Avenue
St. Catharines
Ontario
Canada
L2M 5V6

73 Lime Walk
Headington
Oxford
OX3 7AD
United Kingdom

Cataloging-in-Publication Data
Kalman, Bobbie
  Breakfast blast / Bobbie Kalman.
    p. cm. -- (Kid power)
Includes index.
Explores why and how to have a delicious and healthy breakfast
through nutrition facts and easy recipes for nourishing foods.
  ISBN 0-7787-1250-8 (RLB) -- ISBN 0-7787-1272-9 (pbk)
  1. Breakfasts--Juvenile literature. 2. Cookery, American--Juvenile
literature. [1. Breakfasts. 2. Food habits. 3. Cookery.] I. Title. II. Series.
  TX733.K34 2003
  641.5'2--dc21
                                                    2003001791
                                                    LC

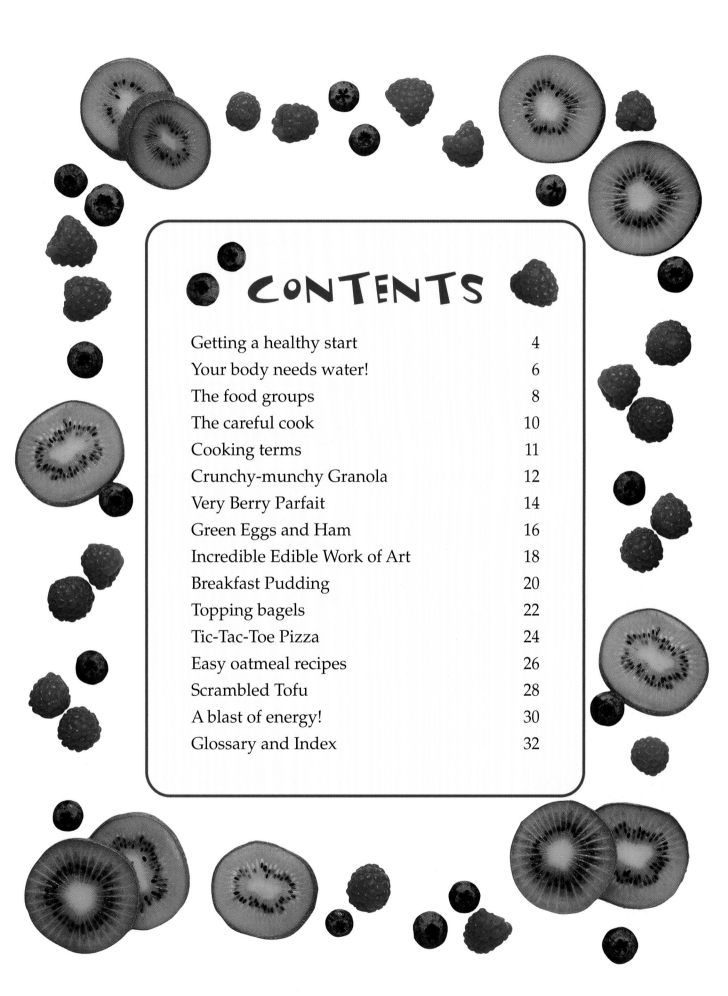

CONTENTS

The word "breakfast" comes from two words—"break" and "fast." After dinner or your last evening snack, you **fast**, or stop eating, until your morning meal. Breakfast breaks the fast! Having a healthy breakfast helps you in three important ways:

1. It gives your body its first **nutrition** and **energy** of the day. Nutrition is the food you eat and the nourishing elements it contains, and energy is the power your body needs to **function**, or work.
2. It improves your ability to concentrate at school and be more creative.
3. It helps you maintain a healthy weight. When you eat breakfast, you are less likely to eat too much the rest of the day.

Decide to be healthy now!

We realize that it is not easy to change your **diet**, or the food you normally eat, all at once, but eating a nutritious breakfast will give you a healthy start each day. The recipes in this book include a variety of foods made from fresh ingredients, which contain more **nutrients** (see page 5) than the **processed** foods you may now be eating. Most processed foods, such as many breakfast cereals, have few nutrients and contain added sugar, salt, fat, and artificial ingredients.

Foods you will love

The kids in this book had fun making our breakfast recipes, but they enjoyed the results even more! They were surprised at how delicious nutritious foods can taste. You'll love these breakfasts, too. Try the recipes with your family and get everyone involved in healthy eating.

Have a blast trying our recipes!

Tips for a healthier you
- Never skip breakfast!
- Drink plenty of water (see pages 6-7).
- Choose a variety of foods each day.
- Choose **whole** grains, which contain many nutrients, over **refined** grains, which have had most of their nutrients removed.
- Eat fresh fruits and vegetables every day.
- Read the labels on processed foods to learn what you are really eating.
- Cut down on sugar, fat, and processed foods.
- Take part in physical activity every day.
- Try some of our breakfast recipes each week.

Nutrients in your food

Nutrients are substances in food that your body needs. The seven essential nutrients, listed in order of importance, are: water, carbohydrates, proteins, fats, vitamins, minerals, and enzymes. Your body needs all seven nutrients to work at its best. Eating a variety of food and drinking plenty of water gives your body and brain maximum power.

Proteins

Proteins are your body's building blocks. They are found in meat, fish and seafood, eggs, milk and soy products, and **legumes**, or dried beans. There are two types of proteins: **complete** and **incomplete**. Complete proteins are in meat, eggs, and milk products. Incomplete proteins are found in beans and grains. When you combine some incomplete proteins, you get a complete protein. Eating a bean salad with whole-grain bread, or brown rice with beans, turns these foods into complete proteins.

Good fats and bad fats

You need fats to make new cells and to **absorb**, or take in, certain vitamins. Fats contained in olive oil, fish, and nuts are good for you. Other fats, such as those found in most processed foods, stop your cells from growing normally. These fats harm your body.

Enzymes

Enzymes are found in all fresh fruits and vegetables, especially in **organic** foods. They are needed by your **digestive** and **metabolic** systems to break down food so your body can absorb the nutrients it needs.

Carbohydrates

Carbohydrates are your body's main source of energy. There are three kinds of carbohydrates—**simple**, **complex**, and **fiber**. Some are better for you than others. Simple carbohydrates are found in sugar and in white-flour products such as cakes. They turn to fat quickly in your body. Simple carbohydrates are also found in fruit and in some vegetables, but these foods also contain fiber and other nutrients your body can use. Whole-grain foods, such as whole-wheat bread, brown rice, and many vegetables, contain complex carbohydrates. These foods release energy more slowly than simple carbohydrates do, so you feel energized for a longer time. Complex carbohydrates also contain fiber, which helps remove wastes from your body.

Vitamins

Vitamins are in all fresh foods. Cooking destroys many vitamins, so it is important to eat some **raw**, or uncooked, vegetables and fruits each day. Vitamins A, C, D, E, and K are essential to your body. They are also important in maintaining a healthy **immune system**, which fights diseases and keeps you from getting sick. Your immune system also helps you heal when you are sick or injured.

Minerals

Minerals include calcium, iron, potassium, magnesium, and zinc. They are as important as vitamins. Calcium, for example, helps build your bones. It is found in milk, meat, almonds, and green vegetables such as broccoli.

YOUR BODY NEEDS WATER!

Water is your most important nutrient—you could not live without it for more than five days! Between 60 and 75 percent of your body is water. Your bones are 22 percent water, your muscles are 70 percent water, your blood is 83 percent water, and your brain is 75 percent water. Without water, your brain, muscles, bones, organs, and **metabolism** stop working! Your metabolism helps change the food you eat into energy.

How your body uses water

Your body's water supply:
• controls your body temperature
• keeps your skin healthy and smooth
• develops your muscles
• helps **lubricate**, or moisten, your food so you can digest it
• lubricates your eyes, nose, mouth, and every joint in your body so you can move
• carries nutrients, energy, and information to and from your cells
• helps your body get rid of waste

The dangers of dehydration

Dehydration means losing water from your body. Being dehydrated can be dangerous! When you are dehydrated, your temperature rises, and your body loses minerals such as sodium and potassium. You can become sick from losing too much water. Dehydration is especially dangerous in hot weather or when you're physically active. Most people are slightly dehydrated all the time and don't even know it. Drink water throughout the day—before you feel thirsty. If you are thirsty, you are already dehydrated!

The best drink by far!
Many people drink sodas when they are thirsty, but they are doing the opposite of what their bodies need. Sodas contain caffeine, which takes water out of your body instead of adding water to it. Each can of soda also contains phosphorous and nine teaspoons of sugar! Too much phosphorous and caffeine can rob your bones of calcium, so if you are drinking sodas every day, your bones may be getting thinner! Vegetable juices, teas, and fruit juices add water to your body, but some contain sugar or salt. The best way to keep your body hydrated is to drink plenty of pure water!

Dehydration warning signs
Do you know the warning signs of dehydration? You might be dehydrated if you...
• are extremely thirsty
• are extremely hungry
• feel light-headed or dizzy
• feel hot
• are unable to concentrate
• have a dry mouth
• feel extremely tired
• are unusually clumsy
• have muscle spasms
• have a headache
• are short of breath
• have a rapid pulse
• have blurred vision
• have pain at the back of your ankles

Drink plenty of water!

You should try to drink at least 6-8 glasses of water a day. This amount sounds like a lot, but these tips can help you drink the water you need.

- Drink one to two glasses of water as soon as you get up in the morning. Add a squirt of lemon juice to your first glass to get your digestive system going. On a cold day, sip some hot water flavored with lemon.
- Sip—don't gulp—a half glass of water every 30 minutes, even when you do not feel thirsty.
- Always drink water before and after exercise. Do not drink ice-cold water or cold liquids when your body is very hot.
- Drink plenty of water when you are working in front of a computer. Computers can dehydrate you quickly.
- If you feel very hungry, you may be thirsty. Drink a glass of water and then see if you are still hungry.
- To make water taste delicious, flavor it with fresh fruit slices, as shown on this page.

Give your body a refreshing blast of water!

1 To make **Orange Water**, wash an orange and cut it in half with its rind on. Cut it again into quarters and then slice the quarters into thirds. Use half an orange to flavor a jug of water. Do not squeeze the orange juice into the water—just drop the pieces into the jug. Allow the water to stand for about 30 minutes. You can refill the jug once using the same orange pieces. Discard the orange pieces after about six hours.

2 To make **Strawberry Water**, wash and slice five or six strawberries and add the pieces to a bottle or pitcher of water. If you want to make only one glass, use one berry. Allow a half hour for the strawberries to flavor the water. Drink the water within six hours and then throw the berries away. You can take the flavored water to school in a bottle.

THE FOOD GROUPS

There are four main **food groups**, or types of food: grain products, vegetables and fruits, milk and **alternatives**, and meat and alternatives. Alternatives are foods that contain the same type of nutrients as those found in another food. Soy beverage, for example, is a milk alternative. Eating foods from different food groups provides your body with a wide variety of nutrients. Your body needs more grains and vegetables and fruits than it needs milk and meat products, however, so eat more from the two food groups on this page. Try to eat as little as possible of the "foods" mentioned in the blue box on page 9.

Grain products

Your body needs a lot of grains. Some grains are better for you than others, however. Whole-grain breads and pastas and brown rice have many nutrients, including fiber, that give you energy for hours. **Refined**, or processed, grain foods are not as good for you because they have had their nutritious parts removed. They act like simple carbohydrates in your body and do not give you long-lasting energy. Refined grains include white rice and flour and foods made from these grains, such as bread, cakes, and many breakfast cereals. Always choose whole grains, such as the bread below left. Refined grain products are usually lighter in color.

whole-wheat bread

white bread

white rice

Vegetables and fruits

Vegetables and fruits are some of the best foods you can eat. They're packed with vitamins and minerals and also contain enzymes. Fruits and vegetables are high in fiber and low in fat. They give you a lot of energy and make you feel full. Have several kinds of fruits and vegetables each day and make sure you eat some of them raw. Remember that french fries, potato chips, and onion rings are not vegetables—they are mostly salt and fat.

Blast your way to good health by eating great food!

Milk products and alternatives

Milk and dairy products provide you with protein, vitamins, and minerals such as calcium. Eating or drinking a milk product every day can also help you maintain a healthy weight. Milk alternatives such as soy beverages and cheeses are rich in protein and calcium, just as milk products are. Whether you choose milk products, soy products, or both, read the labels to see how much fat and sugar they contain. Also beware of artificial colors, flavors, and sweeteners. They are harmful to your body.

milk cheese

soy beverage

milk

tofu

soy cheese

milk cheese

Meat, fish, and alternatives

Meat and fish are great sources of protein, vitamins, and minerals. Fish such as salmon and sardines are especially good for you. Some people do not eat meat or fish, however. They choose alternatives such as eggs, a combination of beans and rice, or soy products such as tofu. Eggs are a wonderful food because they contain important nutrients that are hard to find in other foods. Almonds and peanuts are also considered to be meat alternatives because they contain protein and calcium.

eggs

almonds

meat

tofu

kidney beans

fish

Not part of the four groups

Some foods don't fit into the four food groups. They get lumped together in a group of "other foods." The only healthy foods that belong to this group are good fats such as nuts and olive oil. Most of the "other foods" in this group shouldn't even be called foods because they have very few nutrients. "Junk foods" such as candy, cake, chips, and soda contain **empty calories**, which make you gain weight while starving your body at the same time. When you eat empty calories, your body wants you to keep eating because it is not getting the nutrients it needs. Junk foods may give you a burst of energy, but it doesn't last long! You'll feel tired soon after you eat them. Junk foods also contain a lot of artificial ingredients, too, such as sweeteners. Recent studies show that these ingredients cause many diseases, such as liver disease and cancer.

THE CAREFUL COOK

Cooking is fun, but it can also be dangerous if you are not careful. When you are using the oven, stove, knife, or food processor, make sure there is an adult in the kitchen with you. Accidents such as burns and cuts can happen quickly! **Allergies** are another common food-related problem. Before you start cooking, have an adult who knows your allergies check over each recipe's ingredients. Some foods may contain ingredients such as nut oils. If you are allergic to nuts, be careful to read the labels on foods such as dried fruits and seeds. Nut oils can be found in many processed foods.

What is this girl doing wrong while using a knife? Firstly, she is cutting too close to her fingers. Secondly, she is holding her wrist too high. She would have much better control of the knife with her wrist down, in a straight line from her elbow.

More safety tips

- Before and after handling food, wash with detergent and water all the surfaces on which you are working, such as cutting boards and countertops.
- Next, wash your hands. Always wash your hands with soap and warm water after handling eggs and raw meat. When washing up, include your palms, the backs of your hands, your fingertips and nails, and between your fingers. How long should you wash your hands? As you soap your hands, sing the Happy Birthday song. Do not stop soaping until you have finished. Then rinse with warm water.

- Be sure to wash any raw fruits and vegetables thoroughly before you cook or eat them.
- Always wear oven mitts when you handle anything in the oven.
- Turn the handles of pots and pans away from the edge of the stove so you do not accidentally knock them and spill hot liquid on yourself or others.
- If your hair is long, tie it back so that it does not touch the food or get in the way while you are cooking.

COOKING TERMS

When using the recipes in this book, you may see some cooking **terms**, or special words, that aren't familiar to you. The pictures shown here illustrate some of these terms. The recipes also include metric measurements in brackets. The letter "l" stands for liter, and the letters "ml" mean milliliter. When you see the words **teaspoon**, **tablespoon**, or **cup** without metric amounts beside them, you can use a regular cup, teaspoon, or tablespoon from your kitchen. In fact, many of the ingredients in this book do not have to be exact. We use terms such as **sprinkle**, **dash**, **drizzle**, **pinch**, and **handful**. When you see these words, you can use a bit more or less of an ingredient.

slice, chop: cut food into even pieces

dice: cut food into small squares

core: remove stem and core from the center of fruit

handful: an amount that fits in your hand

drizzle: allow liquid to flow in a thin stream

sauté: stir while cooking over medium heat

whisk together: blend well using a whisk or fork

grate: rub an ingredient against a grater

toothpick test: check to see if food is dry in center

blend: add ingredients while stirring

grease: rub a pan with oil or butter so food won't stick

sprinkle: scatter solid or liquid particles over food

11

CRUNCHY-MUNCHY GRANOLA

Granola is a wonderfully nutritious food that you can use in a number of ways. Enjoy a bowl of granola with low-fat milk or yogurt and fresh fruits such as sliced bananas or berries. Use it to make a Very Berry Parfait (see pages 14-15) or sprinkle some on a fruit salad (see pages 18-19). This recipe does not contain the added fats, salt, refined sugar, or chemicals found in many packaged granolas. Your body will get nutrients such as complex carbohydrates, good fats, minerals, vitamins, and protein—especially when you add milk, yogurt, or a soy beverage. To make this recipe, you do not need to use exact amounts.

To make 12-16 servings, you need:
- 3-4 cups oatmeal
- ½ cup sesame seeds
- ½ cup sunflower seeds
- ½ cup wheat germ
- ½ cup powdered non-fat milk
- ¾ cup unsweetened shredded coconut
- 1 cup chopped nuts (walnuts, almonds, pecans, or a combination)
- ½ cup applesauce
- ½ cup orange or apple juice
- ¼ cup maple syrup or honey
- 2 teaspoons vanilla
- ½ cup raisins, dried cranberries, or other dried fruits

Add the dried fruits after baking—they get hard when they are baked.

1 Preheat oven to 300°F (150°C). Put the first seven ingredients, which are the dry ingredients, into a bowl and stir with a long-handled spoon until they are blended well.

2 Pour the honey or maple syrup, juice, applesauce, and vanilla, which are the wet ingredients, into another bowl and blend well.

3 Pour the wet ingredients into the dry ingredients and blend them until the mixture is moist.

4 Line two large cookie sheets with parchment paper or grease the sheets lightly with sunflower oil.

5 Spread the granola mixture onto the baking pans, as shown on the opposite page. Bake for 30 minutes or until the granola starts turning brown. Wearing oven mitts, stir the granola often with a long-handled spoon while it is baking.

6 Take the granola out of the oven and allow it to cool for about a half hour. It will get nice and crunchy. Put it into a bowl and add raisins or other dried fruits of your choice.

Breakfast Blast taste guarantee: You'll go ga-ga over this great granola!

7 Store the granola in the refrigerator in a glass jar or plastic container. It is so delicious, it will not last long. Your whole family will love it!

13

VERY BERRY PARFAIT

You'll love this delicious breakfast! Not only is it "berry" tasty, but it will also supply your body with a healthy variety of nutrients. Yogurt provides calcium and protein, and the berries and granola are full of vitamins and fiber. The ingredients in this parfait come from three different food groups, helping you get your day off to a great start. Making this breakfast is easy and a lot of fun. When it is finished, it looks so beautiful, you will want to serve it to your family.

For each parfait you need:
- 1 cup (250 ml) plain yogurt or low-fat vanilla yogurt
- 6 fresh strawberries or ½ cup (125 ml) blueberries or raspberries
- ⅓ cup (85 ml) granola (see pages 12-13 for the homemade granola recipe)

1 Wash the strawberries well and pull off their leafy parts.

Give your mouth a refreshing berry blast!

2 Cut the strawberries into bite-sized pieces and put them into a bowl.

3 Cover the bottom of a stemmed glass with a layer of berries. Now add a layer of yogurt.

4 Sprinkle half of the granola over the yogurt. Repeat the layers by adding more fruit and yogurt. Top with the remaining granola.

This recipe will be one of your favorites. It is a nutritious breakfast that tastes more like a delicious dessert!

GREEN EGGS AND HAM

Eggs are quick and easy to make and can be cooked in a variety of ways. You can boil eggs, fry them, poach them, scramble them, or make them into omelets. This recipe was inspired by Dr. Seuss's famous children's book *Green Eggs and Ham*. Our "green eggs" contain healthy green vegetables, and the "ham" is Canadian bacon, which has much less fat than other types of ham. Although both eggs and ham are loaded with protein, ham contains chemicals that are not good for you, so don't eat it too often. Try this recipe for Green Eggs and Ham and think of other healthy green veggies you can use to make your own version of "green eggs."

For two servings you need:
- 2 eggs
- about a tablespoon of each of the following green vegetables: green onions, celery, spinach, green peppers, and herbs such as parsley, dill, or chives
- 1 teaspoon (5 ml) cooking oil
- 2 pieces of Canadian bacon
- salt and pepper to taste

1 Break the eggs one at a time against the edge of a bowl or counter. Drop the inside of the eggs into a cup or small bowl and throw out the shells.

2 Whisk together the eggs with a fork, as shown left. Set them aside.

3 Wash all your vegetables well and slice them into bite-sized pieces.

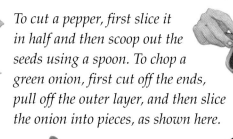

To cut a pepper, first slice it in half and then scoop out the seeds using a spoon. To chop a green onion, first cut off the ends, pull off the outer layer, and then slice the onion into pieces, as shown here.

Warning!
Raw eggs contain harmful bacteria such as salmonella, which can make you very sick. Always wash your hands after handling eggs—even eggshells—and wash the counters, too. Make sure you cook your eggs well.

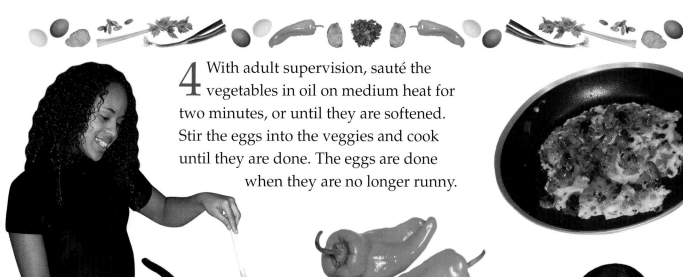

4 With adult supervision, sauté the vegetables in oil on medium heat for two minutes, or until they are softened. Stir the eggs into the veggies and cook until they are done. The eggs are done when they are no longer runny.

5 Prepare the Canadian bacon by placing it in a frying pan with a little water. Heat over medium heat for about two minutes on each side.

6 Put the eggs on a green **serving** plate and share them with a family member. There is enough food for two.

7 To make your eggs even greener, serve them with some lettuce greens and cucumber slices.

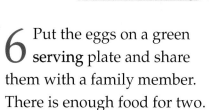

17

INCREDIBLE EDIBLE WORK OF ART

Fruit salad is a fresh, tasty breakfast that gets your day off to a healthy start. Fruit contains many nutrients, including vitamins, enzymes, and fiber. Berries are particularly good for preventing diseases and helping your eyes. Look at the salad on the right to get ideas for your own work of edible art. How many colors can you add? Use your imagination!

You need:
Three or more types of fruit such as: kiwis, strawberries, oranges, grapes, watermelon, cantaloupe, blueberries, or raspberries. Look at the fruit bowl above for some great ideas.

1 Wash your fruit carefully before peeling or cutting it.

2 Ask an adult to **score** an orange, or cut into its rind, so you can peel it easily, as shown below left. Remove the rind.

3 Cut the orange into thin slices, as shown here.

4 Cut a kiwi in half and remove the peel before you slice it, or slice it first and then peel each piece.

5 Add as many kinds of sliced fruits as you like, but make sure you can eat or share what you make. Add a spoonful of vanilla yogurt and some nuts to the fruit, if you wish.

This sensational salad will wow your eyes and blast your tastebuds awake!

BREAKFAST PUDDING

If you're tired of toast or cereal in the morning, try this pudding for a hearty, hot breakfast. You can prepare some of the ingredients the night before and put the pudding together when you get up in the morning. This breakfast provides you with protein and complex carbohydrates to give you plenty of energy. The meat and veggies in this recipe taste great together, but you can try other combinations, too. Apples and onions are delicious with ham.

For one serving you need:

- 1 slice of whole-grain bread
- 1 slice of ham or ½ piece of pre-cooked bacon (optional)
- ½ cup (125 ml) of one or ¼ cup (62 ml) of two of each of the following fruits, vegetables, or herbs: green pepper, mushroom, onion, tomato, zucchini, apple, and parsley
- ¼ cup (62 ml) grated cheese
- 1 egg, beaten
- ¼ cup (62 ml) milk
- a pinch of salt
- a sprinkle of nutmeg

1 Preheat the oven to 350°F (180°C). Lightly grease a small baking dish. Tear the bread into pieces and put the pieces into the dish.

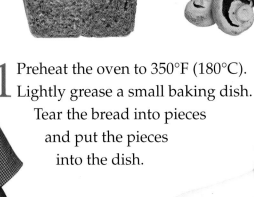

2 Put the bacon or ham pieces on top of the bread. Chop the fruits, vegetables, or herbs into bite-sized pieces and layer them on top of the ham. If you are using onion, mushroom, pepper, or zucchini pieces, sauté them first in a teaspoon of oil.

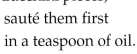

3 Sprinkle the cheese on top of the vegetables. Whisk together the egg, milk, and salt. Pour the mixture over the other ingredients. Sprinkle with a little nutmeg.

4 Bake for 40 to 50 minutes or until the pudding is puffed up and golden. Do a toothpick test to make sure it is done in the center. The toothpick should come out clean.

5 Serve the pudding with tomato or pepper slices and lettuce greens.

TOPPING BAGELS

No matter what your tastes are, there's a bagel for you! There are plain bagels, bagels with seeds on top, cinnamon-and-raisin bagels, and cheese-and-onion bagels, just to name a few. Whole-grain bagels such as whole-wheat bagels and multi-grain bagels have more nutrients than many other types because they contain complex carbohydrates. What you put on your bagel will also make a difference to your body. Butter and jam are high in fat and sugar and do not contain many of the nutrients your body needs. Cream cheese is a better choice because it contains protein and calcium. Adding some fresh fruit or canned fruit makes this topping extra tasty. Natural peanut butter with no added salt or sugar is also a nutritious topping, if you are not allergic to peanuts!

You need:
- a bagel
- a small container of cream cheese
- ¼ cup (62 ml) fresh fruit or fruit canned in juice such as peaches

1 Buy bagels that are pre-cut or ask an adult to slice them for you. Bagels can be tricky to cut!

2 Use spreadable cream cheese or take regular cream cheese out of the refrigerator and allow it to soften for about half an hour.

3 Cut the fruit into bite-sized pieces. If you're using canned fruit, drain it first. In a bowl, blend the fruit into the cream cheese.

4 Spread a thin layer of the cream-cheese mixture on your bagel and enjoy. Watch out for the dreaded cheese moustache!

5 To make a peanut-apple-honey topping, spread peanut butter on your bagel. Core an apple and cut some thin slices. Arrange the apple slices on top of the peanut butter.

Yummy!

6 Drizzle a tiny bit of honey over the apple slices.

23

TiC-TAC-TOE Pizza

The toppings on this pizza look like a game of Tic-Tac-Toe, which is how this pizza got it name. It is fun to make and is also good for you. It contains something from each food group. Prepare the pizza the night before but don't add the fruit until morning. The pizza takes only a few minutes to bake.

For one pizza you need:
- one pocketless pita bread (preferably a whole-grain pita)
- a handful of grated cheese (swiss, mozzarella, or cheddar)
- a slice of ham
- 4-6 small pineapple chunks
- some raisins or dried cranberries
- a parsley leaf

1 To prepare the ham, cut it into strips with a pizza cutter or knife.

2 Buy some grated cheese or grate your own. Watch your fingers!

3 Take a handful of grated cheese and spread it over the pizza. Lay down four strips of ham, as shown below. Put a leaf of parsley in the center. Add the fruit just before you bake the pizza.

4 Preheat the oven to 400°F (200°C). Place the pizza on a pizza pan or baking sheet. Using oven mitts, put the pizza into the oven. Bake for ten minutes.

Pizza for breakfast? What a blast!

5 When the cheese has melted, your pizza is done. Wearing oven mitts, remove the pizza from the oven and enjoy this tasty breakfast!

EASY OATMEAL RECIPES

People say that oatmeal "sticks to your ribs," which means you will not feel hungry for a long time after you eat it. If your belly starts growling during your morning classes, oatmeal is the breakfast for you! It is a good source of energy and fiber. Most people cook their oatmeal, but you don't have to if you use these two recipes. Both are eaten cold with fruit and some yogurt. The first recipe uses "minute" or quick-cook oats. The second recipe, which is also known as "muesli," calls for slow-cook oats. You need to prepare both recipes the night before.

For one serving you need:
- ½ cup (125 ml) plain yogurt
- ½ cup (125 ml) quick-cook oats
- 1 tablespoon (15 ml) orange juice
- ¼ cup (62 ml) canned peach pieces
- ground cinnamon (optional)
- ground nutmeg (optional)
- half an unpeeled apple, washed, cored, and chopped into bite-sized pieces
- ¼ cup (62 ml) chopped walnuts
- 1 teaspoon (5 ml) maple syrup

Fruity Oatmeal

1 Put the yogurt into a bowl and spoon in the oats and orange juice. Cut the peach slices into bite-sized pieces and add. Stir the mixture well.

2 Sprinkle on some cinnamon and nutmeg and cover the mixture with plastic wrap. Refrigerate overnight to allow the flavors to blend together.

3 Just before eating, cut the apple into bite-sized pieces and add it to the oatmeal. Sprinkle the nuts on top of the oatmeal and drizzle with maple syrup. Enjoy this healthy and amazing breakfast!

Muesli Recipe

1 Place the oats in a bowl and add enough hot water to cover them. Cover the bowl and place it in the refrigerator overnight.

2 In the morning, slice some fresh fruit, or add dried fruit, and mix it into the oats.

3 Add the yogurt, honey or maple syrup, nuts, vanilla, and cinnamon. Stir the mixture and get ready for a delicious taste experience!

For one serving you need:
- ½ cup (125 ml) slow-cook oats
- about 2 tablespoons of any of the following fruits: apples, pears, bananas, berries, or canned peaches (You can also use dried fruit such as raisins or chopped pitted prunes.)
- 2 tablespoons (30 ml) low-fat yogurt
- a drizzle of honey or maple syrup
- a sprinkle of cinnamon
- a handful of chopped nuts
- ½ teaspoon (2.5 ml) vanilla

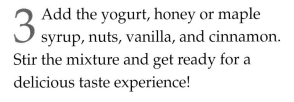

SCRAMBLED TOFU

You may think you don't like tofu, but we bet you've never tasted tofu like this! Tofu is a source of calcium and an excellent alternative for people who are allergic to milk products. It is also a source of protein and can be as a meat or egg substitute. In this recipe, we are using tofu as an egg substitute. On its own, tofu has almost no flavor, but it takes on the flavor of whatever you add to it or cook with it. Silken tofu is used to make smoothies and desserts, and firm tofu is used in stir-fries and **casseroles**, or one-dish meals.

For one serving you need:
- ½ cup (125 ml) firm tofu
- about 2 tablespoons (30 ml) of each of the following: diced red onion, chopped red or yellow pepper, sliced celery, grated carrots, and chopped parsley
- ½ small diced tomato
- 1 teaspoon olive oil
- a dash of salt and cumin or chili powder

1 Wash the vegetables well and chop the onion, pepper, tomato, celery, and parsley into bite-sized pieces.

(below) To chop parsley, first slice it one way and then turn it slightly and slice again. You can also use scissors to cut off the leaves.

2 Put the oil into a frying pan and then add the onion and parsley. Sauté over medium heat for three minutes or until the onions are soft.

3 Rinse and drain the tofu. Crumble it by squeezing it through your fingers. Add it to the pan along with the salt and cumin.

4 Add the pepper, celery, carrot, and tomato and sauté until the tofu has absorbed the juices and flavors of the vegetables—about 2 to 3 minutes. To make a more complete meal, enjoy your tofu with a piece of whole-grain toast. Yummy!

29

A BLAST OF ENERGY!

Eating a good breakfast is the right way to start your day. There are other things you can do as well to kick-start your body and brain so you have a great day at school.

1 To do some good things for your health, get up fifteen minutes earlier than you normally would.

2 Drink a glass or two of water with lemon to nourish your body and get your digestive system ready for breakfast.

3 Now do some stretches to wake up your body. If it is warm outside, do your stretches outdoors and get some sunshine at the same time. Sunshine will give you an extra blast of energy.

4 To bring the sun's energy into your body, stretch your arms and fingers as high as you can. Imagine that the sun's rays are entering your body through your fingertips and traveling right down to your toes.

5 Bend backward as far as you can and breathe air deep into your lungs. You will stretch your chest muscles at the same time.

6 Stretch one side of your body and then the other by bending sideways.

7 On your knees, round your back and then arch it, as a cat would do.

8 Still on your knees, bend forward and stretch out your back, arms, and shoulders.

9 If you can, walk up and down the stairs a few times or run around the block.

10
Decide what you want to eat for breakfast and start preparing it. Never skip this important meal! Here are some breakfast menus using the recipes in this book and some other basic ingredients.

Menu 6
• Scrambled Tofu and a slice of whole-wheat toast
• a glass of Strawberry Water
(See pages 7, 28-29.)

Menu 1
• Tic-Tac-Toe Pizza
• a glass of juice
(See pages 24-25.)

Menu 2
• a half cup of oatmeal
• a cup of fruit salad
(See pages 18-19, 26.)

Menu 7
• Very Berry Parfait
• a glass of juice
(See pages 14-15.)

Menu 3
• Green Eggs and Ham
• a piece of whole-grain toast
• a glass of juice
(See pages 16-17.)

Quick breakfasts
• a half bagel and cream cheese with a glass of milk or juice
or
• 2 slices of whole-wheat toast with sliced tomatoes and cheese and a glass of juice

Menu 4
• a cup of granola with milk and a half cup of berries
(See pages 12-13.)

Menu 5
• Breakfast Pudding
• veggie slices
• Orange Water
(See pages 7, 20-21.)

31

GLOSSARY

Note: Words that have been defined in the book may not appear in the glossary. (Also see page 11 for cooking terms.)

allergy A negative reaction to certain foods

alternative A food that provides the same nutrients as another food

casserole A meal with several ingredients, which are all cooked in the same dish

dehydration A dangerous lack of fluids in the body due to not drinking enough water or losing too much body fluid

digestive system A system of organs in the body that helps break down food

food groups Foods that have been divided into categories according to type

immune system A body system that fights disease and helps the body heal

legumes Dried beans

metabolic system (metabolism) A body system that changes nutrients into energy

organic Describing foods grown or prepared without the use of harmful pesticides

processed foods Foods to which sugar, color, or other chemicals have been added

whole grains Grains that have not been refined, or had their nutritous parts removed

INDEX

1 2 3 4 5 6 7 8 9 0 Printed in the U.S.A. 2 1 0 9 8 7 6 5 4 3